Betty Crocker

Diabetes

WILEY

Wiley Publishing, Inc.

General Mills

Editorial Director: Jeff Nowak

Publishing Manager: Christine Gray

Editor: Grace Wells

Recipe Development and Testing: Betty Crocker Kitchens

Photography: General Mills Photography Studios and Image Library

International Diabetes Center

Richard M. Bergenstal, M.D., Endocrinologist

Diane Reader, R.D., L.D., C.D.E.

Maureen Doran, R.D., L.D.

Wiley Publishing, Inc.

Publisher: Natalie Chapman

Executive Editor: Anne Ficklen

Editor: Meaghan McDonnell

Production Manager: Michael Olivo

Cover Design: Suzanne Sunwoo

Art Director: Tai Blanche

Layout: Indianapolis Composition Services

Manufacturing Manager: Kevin Watt

The Betty Crocker Kitchens seal guarantees success in your kitchen. Every recipe has been tested in America's Most Trusted Kitchens™ to meet our high standards of reliability, easy preparation and great taste.

FIND MORE GREAT IDEAS AT

BettyCrocker.com

This book is printed on acid-free paper. ♾

For general information on our other products and services or for technical support, please contact our Customer Care Department within the United States at (877) 762-2974, outside the United States at (317) 572-3993 or fax (317) 572-4002.

Wiley also publishes its books in a variety of electronic formats. Some content that appears in print may not be available in electronic books. For more information about Wiley products, visit our web site at www.wiley.com.

ISBN-13: 978-0-470-64721-9

Manufactured in China

10 9 8 7 6 5 4 3 2 1

Cover photos (from left to right): Italian Shrimp Stir-Fry (page 46), Baked Chicken and Rice with Autumn Vegetables (page 40), and Creamy Vanilla-Caramel Cheesecake (page 90)

At Betty Crocker, we know it is possible to live well with diabetes. To make your life easier, Betty Crocker teamed up with the International Diabetes Center to create great recipes and offer you sound advice. This book offers easy, delicious recipes the whole family will enjoy and provides reliable medical and nutritional information essential for people with diabetes.

Warm Regards,

Betty Crocker

CONTENTS

Living Well with Diabetes

The best-kept secret about diabetes food planning is that it is good for virtually everyone. You may think that people with diabetes need special foods prepared special ways, but as you look through this book, you may be surprised to see the wide variety of delicious and satisfying foods that you can eat. The key is moderation.

Carbohydrate Choices

If you have diabetes, you've come to the right place—this cookbook offers the latest and easiest way to count Carbohydrate Choices. These guidelines are easier than the exchange system because you only need to keep track of one thing: the amount of carbohydrate that you eat for each meal and snack. If you're used to keeping track of food exchanges, that information is included for you, too.

To create this cookbook, we've enlisted the experienced help of an endocrinologist (a diabetes specialist doctor) and two diabetes dietitians who have many years of experience working with people with diabetes. Teamed with the trusted recipes of the Betty Crocker Kitchens, you're sure to use and refer to this cookbook again and again.

The recipes in this cookbook were developed for healthy eating with diabetes, and each recipe lists the Carbohydrate Choices per serving, removing the guesswork for you. Keeping overall health and all-family appeal in mind, we've kept the fat, sugar and calories down, added whole grains, boosted the fiber and used a variety of spices and herbs to keep the lid on sodium without sacrificing the naturally delicious satisfying flavor of the food.

A diagnosis of diabetes may make you feel like your life is spinning out of control. One positive way to approach this news is to think of having diabetes as an opportunity to take charge of your health and find great pleasure in the foods you select and eat. Whether you've been recently diagnosed with diabetes, have been living with it for a while or are giving care to someone with diabetes, this book is your helpful tool on the road to better health.

Along with having great food options, it's important to know as much as you can about diabetes, how to take good care of yourself and how your diabetes care team can help you. This cookbook is packed with information that will guide you in taking the best possible care of your diabetes. The basics of good nutrition and a detailed explanation of how to use carbohydrate counting for food planning follows. Read it now, or use it as a refresher later. It's all right at your fingertips!

Who's at Greater Risk?

As the incidence of diabetes grows, more is understood about the disease and who is at risk. Regular testing is recommended for anyone who:

- Has a family member with diabetes, especially type 2 diabetes

- Is of African American, Hispanic American, Native American, Southeast Asian or Pacific Islander heritage

- Has had gestational diabetes or a baby weighing more than nine pounds at birth

- Leads a sedentary or inactive lifestyle

- Has components of the "metabolic syndrome," which includes abnormal blood lipids (high triglycerides and low HDL—or "good"—cholesterol), high blood pressure, obesity, insulin resistance and polycystic ovary syndrome in women.

Diabetes Nutrition 101

The primary goal in diabetes care is blood glucose control, followed closely by the need to control blood fats and blood pressure, and to minimize weight gain, all of which play a significant role in diabetes health.

At the foundation of achieving all of these goals is good nutrition. A nutritious, well-balanced diet provides the building blocks for healthy body functioning, physical energy, satisfaction in eating and just feeling good!

Carbohydrate Counting

Carbohydrate is measured in grams. A gram is a small unit of weight in the metric system. The trick to carbohydrate counting is to know how many carbohydrate grams you are eating at any given time. Carbohydrate counting provides you with a tool to help with blood glucose control and enables you to select the amount of carbohydrate recommended by your healthcare provider for a well-balanced diet. Research is underway to further define the proper mix of protein, fat and carbohydrate to help a person maintain optimal health.

A typical diabetes food plan includes 3 to 5 Carbohydrate Choices (see "What Is a Carbohydrate Choice?" on page 12) for meals, depending upon your gender and food planning goals. Snacks are usually 1 to 2 Choices, if they are included in your plan. You and your dietitian will determine how much carbohydrate you should eat each day. Then together, you will find the best way to space carbohydrate foods throughout the day so that you get the energy you need without overwhelming your body's insulin supply. Or, if you take insulin, your diabetes care provider will help determine the right doses to match the amount of carbohydrate food you eat. Every meal and snack needs to include carbohydrate foods, because that is what your body "runs" on.

It's best to follow your food plan. "Saving" Carbohydrate Choices from one meal or snack to have at another time can lead to low or high blood glucose levels. If you want to eat more than your food plan calls for, you'll need to make up for it with extra exercise or additional insulin.

Your dietitian can tell you more about eating "outside" your food plan. But be careful—eating more of any food adds calories and potentially weight, whether you have diabetes or not.

Carbohydrate on Food Labels

While there are many "standard" 1-Carbohydrate-Choice foods, such as milk, fruit and bread, you may also want to eat carbohydrate-containing foods such as pizza, frozen dinners or frozen yogurt. How do these foods translate into Carbohydrate Choices? Look to the nutrition label on the food package.

Nutrition labels on packaged foods provide the carbohydrate content of that specific product. Finding the carbohydrate on a Nutrition Facts panel of a food package is easy. Begin by looking at the serving size of the food. Looking down the panel, locate the carbohydrate grams for that serving. "Total Carbohydrate" includes all starches, sugars and dietary fiber.

You can use the "How Many Carbohydrate Choices?" conversion guide (page 10) to convert the number of carbohydrate grams on any label to the number of Carbohydrate Choices.

Nutrition Facts	
Serving Size 1 cup (228g)	
Servings Per Container 2	
Amount Per Serving	
Calories 250	Calories from Fat 110
	% Daily Value*
Total Fat 12g	18%
Saturated Fat 3g	15%
Trans Fat 1.5g	
Cholesterol 30mg	10%
Sodium 470mg	20%
Total Carbohydrate 31g	10%
Dietary Fiber 0g	0%
Sugars 5g	
Protein 5g	
Vitamin A	4%
Vitamin C	2%
Calcium	20%
Iron	4%

* Percent Daily Values are based on a 2,000 calorie diet. Your Daily Values may be higher or lower depending on your calorie needs:

		Calories:	2,000	2,500
Total Fat	Less than		65g	80g
Sat Fat	Less than		20g	25g
Cholesterol	Less than		300mg	300mg
Sodium	Less than		2,400mg	2,400mg
Total Carbohydrate			300g	375g
Dietary Fiber			25g	30g

How Many Carbohydrate Choices?

Use this conversion guide to convert the number of carbohydrate grams to Carbohydrate Choices. If a food has 5 or more grams of fiber, subtract the total grams of fiber from the total carbohydrate before determining the Carbohydrate Choices. (See Fiber, page 15, for more information.)

Carbohydrate Choices	Total Carbohydrate Grams (g)
0	0–5
½	6–10
1	11–20
1 ½	21–25
2	26–35
2 ½	36–40
3	41–50
3 ½	51–55
4	56–65
4 ½	66–70
5	71–80

Used with permission from International Diabetes Center, Minneapolis, MN

What About Sugar?

Sugar is a carbohydrate. It affects your blood glucose in the same way that other carbohydrates do. Contrary to what many believe, people with diabetes can eat some sweets and foods with added sugar as long as the carbohydrate is counted.

Desserts and tempting sweets can pack a big carbohydrate wallop—even small portions. If you decide to eat a food with added sugar, you need to plan by substituting it for other carbohydrates in your food plan. For example, a two-inch-square piece of cake with frosting has the same amount of carbohydrate as one cup of corn or two slices of bread, but it also contains more fat and calories than the corn or the bread.

Often, foods high in added sugar have little or no nutritional value other than calories. And usually, where there is sugar, there is also fat, so it makes good sense to monitor the sweets you eat.

About Exchange Lists

If you've had diabetes for a while, you may have learned to use the Exchange Lists. If so, you already know a lot about food groups and counting. What's the advantage of Carbohydrate Choices over diet (food) exchanges? Carbohydrate counting is an easier way to manage the food you eat and offers you more flexibility in food selection, making meal planning easier. If you'd like to make the switch to counting Carbohydrate Choices, you'll probably find it much easier than the exchange system.

Carbohydrate Counting Tips

- A good start is to remember that 15 grams of carbohydrate is 1 Choice.

- One starch, fruit or milk exchange is equal to 1 Carbohydrate Choice. All the foods in these three groups raise blood glucose the same.

- Meats and fats aren't counted because they do not contain carbohydrate.

- Nonstarchy vegetables (any vegetable except corn, peas, squash and potatoes) are not counted unless eaten in large (3 cups raw or 1½ cups cooked) quantities.

- If a food has 5 or more grams of fiber, subtract the total grams of fiber from the total carbohydrate before determining the Carbohydrate Choices.

What Is a Carbohydrate Choice?

A Carbohydrate Choice is a serving of food that contains **15 grams of carbohydrate.** This is the approximate amount of carbohydrate in one serving of: **Potato, Rice, Bread, Cereal, Milk, Apple.**

1 Carbohydrate Choice = **1** = **15 grams of Carbohydrate**

If you eat two apples, it counts as 2 Carbohydrate Choices. If you eat one slice of bread and one cup of milk that also counts as 2 Carbohydrate Choices. Your customized food plan will include the right number of Carbohydrate Choices for you.

Essential Nutrients for Good Health

In addition to carbohydrate, there are several nutrients needed every day to maintain optimal health. It's important to balance your intake of proteins and fat as well as carbohydrates as part of a healthy diet. Just as eating too much carbohydrate may lead to excess calories and weight, a diet that's too high in protein and fat but low in carbohydrate won't provide your body with the energy and balanced nutrition it needs for proper functioning. The bottom line is moderation. Low-fat meat and dairy products (with an emphasis on increasing monounsaturated fats) along with a moderate amount of nutritious carbohydrate foods that fit your food plan are the keys to healthy, satisfying eating.

Protein is found in meats, poultry, fish, milk and other dairy products, eggs, dried peas and beans and nuts. Starch and vegetables also have small amounts of protein. Your body uses protein for growth and maintenance. Protein provides four calories per gram. Most Americans eat more protein than their bodies need. Your dietitian will help you determine how much protein is right for your body. Five to seven ounces of protein foods per day are typically recommended. Choosing low-fat meats and dairy products also offers heart-healthy benefits to people with diabetes.

Fat is found in butter, margarine, oils, salad dressings, nuts, seeds, cheese, meat, fish, poultry, snack foods, ice cream, cookies and many desserts. Your body needs some fat for good nutrition, just as it needs protein and carbohydrate. But certain types of fat are better for you than others. There are three different types of fat: monounsaturated, polyunsaturated and saturated. Unsaturated fats are sometimes hydrogenated (hydrogen is added to them) to help make them solid at room temperature. This process creates trans fatty acids. Health professionals recommend eating less saturated and trans fats. These are found in meats; dairy products; coconut, palm and palm kernel oils; partially hydrogenated oils and fats that are hard at room temperature such as butter, shortening and margarine. Saturated fats and trans fats have been proven to raise blood cholesterol levels and can contribute to heart disease. The best choice is monounsaturated fat, which has been shown to improve the cardiovascular system. Monounsaturated fat is found in canola oil, olive oil, nuts and avocados. Polyunsaturated fat, found in corn oil, soybean oil and sunflower oil, is also a better choice than saturated fat.

Fat provides nine calories per gram. This is more than twice the calories found in carbohydrate or protein. Excess calories from fat are very easily stored in the body as fat and can lead to weight gain. It's not healthy to completely cut fats from your diet, especially monounsaturated fats. But most people can afford to reduce the amount of calories they get from fat. Two of the best steps you can take are to reduce your fat intake and to switch to a more beneficial type of fat.

Make Wise Food Choices a Habit

These tips are based on sound nutrition principles and are good for everyone—with or without diabetes.

- **Don't Skip Meals.** For many reasons you may be tempted to skip meals. This isn't a good idea, particularly if you have diabetes. When you skip meals, maintaining stable blood glucose levels becomes difficult. To make matters worse, people usually end up overeating at the next meal. So stick to your food plan, and for those days when that's not possible, talk to your dietitian to find appropriate snack choices to hold you over until your next meal.

- **Plan Meals and Snacks.** Planning what to eat for meals and snacks may seem overwhelming at first, but in time, you'll become an expert on what foods work best for you. If you don't plan, you may find yourself eating whatever is available, which may not be the best foods for you. Before you go shopping, decide on healthy meals and snacks to eat at home or take to work or school for the upcoming week.

- **Eat a Variety of Foods.** Grains, fruits and vegetables are packed with vitamins, minerals and fiber. Foods differ in their nutrient content, so eat a variety of colors and kinds, and be sure to include protein in your daily diet. Variety helps to ensure that your body gets the nutrients it needs for good health. Variety also helps to avoid boredom, which often leads to poor control.

- **Choose Low-Fat Foods Often.** Whenever you have the choice, drink fat-free (skim) milk, eat low-fat cheeses, yogurt and puddings, and use low-fat ingredients for cooking and baking, such as yogurt and light sour cream. Also, choose lean meats and remove the skin from chicken. When buying processed foods, look for those that contain 3 grams of fat or less per 100 calories.

Fiber is necessary to maintain a healthy digestive tract and to help lower blood cholesterol levels. Experts recommend at least 25 grams of fiber daily. To get enough fiber each day, include:

- Bran cereals or whole-grain breads, cereals, rice, pasta and other whole-grain products
- Vegetables and fruits, especially those with edible skins, seeds and hulls
- Legumes (dried beans and peas) and nuts

Foods high in fiber are a good choice. If a food has 5 or more grams of fiber, you can subtract the total grams of fiber from the total carbohydrate before determining the number of Carbohydrate Choices. Your best bet for finding high-fiber packaged foods are cereals, foods with bran and beans.

Water is essential for good health. Experts generally recommend eight to ten glasses of water daily for healthy individuals who do not have trouble with eliminating fluids from the body. Drink even more when it's hot, you're exercising or you don't feel well.

Vitamins help release energy from the fuel sources of carbohydrate, protein and fat. Your vision, hair, skin and the strength of your bones all depend on the vitamins that come from the foods you eat. The more variety you have in your diet, the more likely you are to get all the vitamins your body needs.

Minerals help your body with many functions. Iron, for example, carries much-needed oxygen to your body cells. Calcium is key to strong bones and teeth, and potassium is important for proper nerve and muscle function. Magnesium is also very important for proper body functioning and is often deficient in people with diabetes. The best way to get enough of the minerals you need is through a varied diet, although people with certain health conditions, including people with diabetes, sometimes need a supplement. It's a good idea to check with your healthcare provider about your individual needs.

Nutrition in the Recipes

In addition to the number of Carbohydrate Choices, each recipe in this cookbook lists the calories, calories from fat, fat, saturated fat, cholesterol, sodium, carbohydrate, dietary fiber and protein per serving. Food exchanges are also listed on each recipe. Based on criteria set by the American Dietetic Association and the American Diabetes Association, exchanges are listed as whole or half. To calculate the nutrition content of recipes, these guidelines were followed:

- The first ingredient is used whenever a choice is given (such as ⅓ cup plain yogurt or sour cream).

- The first ingredient amount is used whenever a range is given (such as 2 to 3 teaspoons).

- The first serving number is used whenever a range is given (such as 4 to 6 servings).

- "If desired" ingredients are not included in the nutrition calculations, whether mentioned in the ingredient list or in the recipe directions as a suggestion (such as "top with sour cream if desired").

- Only the amount of a marinade or frying oil that is absorbed during preparation is calculated.

Orange Teriyaki Beef with Noodles, page 49

Key Lime Fruit Salad, page 84

Day-Starter Breakfasts

Country Ham and Asparagus Bake

1
Carbohydrate
Choices

Prep Time: 20 Minutes   **Start to Finish:** 50 Minutes   **8 servings**

1½ cups chopped fully cooked ham
1 medium onion, chopped (½ cup)
¼ cup chopped bell pepper
1 package (10 ounces) frozen asparagus or broccoli cuts
8 eggs or 2 cups fat-free cholesterol-free egg product
2 cups fat-free (skim) milk
1 cup all-purpose flour
¼ cup grated Parmesan cheese
½ teaspoon salt
½ teaspoon pepper
½ teaspoon dried tarragon leaves
1 cup shredded Cheddar cheese (4 ounces)

1 Heat oven to 425°F. Generously grease bottom and sides of rectangular baking dish, 13 × 9 × 2 inches, with shortening or cooking spray. Sprinkle ham, onion, bell pepper and frozen asparagus in baking dish.

2 Beat eggs, milk, flour, Parmesan cheese, salt, pepper and tarragon with fork or wire whisk in medium bowl until smooth; pour over ham mixture.

3 Bake uncovered about 20 minutes or until knife inserted in center comes out clean. Sprinkle with Cheddar cheese. Bake 3 to 5 minutes or until cheese is melted. Let stand 5 minutes before cutting.

Note from Dr. B An easy way to cut calories is to use low-fat or fat-free dairy products, which contain half the calories of regular-fat dairy products. You can use reduced-fat Cheddar cheese in this easy recipe.

1 SERVING: Calories 290; Fat 14g (Saturated 7g); Cholesterol 250mg; Sodium 780mg; Carbohydrate 19g (Dietary Fiber 1g); Protein 22g **Food Exchanges:** 1 Starch; 2 Medium-Fat Meat; 1 Vegetable; 1 Fat

Vegetables and Cheese Frittata

Prep Time: 10 Minutes   **Start to Finish:** 25 Minutes   **6 servings**

0 Carbohydrate Choices

8 eggs or 2 cups fat-free cholesterol-free egg product
½ teaspoon salt
⅛ teaspoon pepper
½ cup shredded Swiss cheese (2 ounces)
2 tablespoons canola oil or butter
2 medium bell peppers, chopped (2 cups)
1 medium onion, chopped (½ cup)

1 Beat eggs, salt and pepper in medium bowl with fork or wire whisk until well mixed. Stir in cheese; set aside.

2 Heat oil in ovenproof 10-inch nonstick skillet over medium heat. Cook bell peppers and onion in oil, stirring occasionally, until onion is tender. Pour egg mixture over pepper mixture. Cover and cook over medium-low heat 8 to 10 minutes or until eggs are set and light brown on bottom.

3 Set oven control to broil. Broil frittata with top 4 to 6 inches from heat about 2 minutes or until golden brown. Cut into wedges.

Note from Dr. B Because blood glucose levels can vary at different times of the day, test your blood glucose throughout the day, not just in the morning. Good times to check it are before lunch or two hours after dinner.

1 SERVING: Calories 190; Fat 14g (Saturated 4g); Cholesterol 300mg; Sodium 330mg; Carbohydrate 5g (Dietary Fiber 1g); Protein 12g **Food Exchanges:** 1½ Medium-Fat Meat; 1 Vegetable

Potato, Bacon and Egg Scramble

1½
Carbohydrate
Choices

Prep Time: 10 Minutes **Start to Finish:** 20 Minutes **5 servings**

1 pound small red potatoes (6 or 7), cubed
6 eggs or 1½ cups fat-free cholesterol-free egg product
⅓ cup fat-free (skim) milk
¼ teaspoon salt
⅛ teaspoon pepper
2 tablespoons canola oil or butter
4 medium green onions, sliced (¼ cup)
5 slices bacon, crisply cooked and crumbled

1 Heat 1 inch water to boiling in 2-quart saucepan. Add potatoes. Cover and heat to boiling; reduce heat to medium-low. Cover and cook 6 to 8 minutes or until potatoes are tender; drain.

2 Beat eggs, milk, salt and pepper with fork or wire whisk until well mixed; set aside.

3 Heat oil in 10-inch skillet over medium-high heat. Cook potatoes in oil 3 to 5 minutes, turning potatoes occasionally, until light brown. Stir in onions. Cook 1 minute, stirring constantly.

4 Pour egg mixture over potato mixture. As egg mixture begins to set at bottom and side, gently lift cooked portions with spatula so that thin, uncooked portion can flow to bottom; avoid constant stirring. Cook 3 to 4 minutes or until eggs are thickened throughout but still moist. Sprinkle with bacon.

Betty's Success Tip A breakfast of eggs, potatoes and bacon can still fit in your life; the key is moderation and counting carbohydrates. At only 1½ Carbohydrate Choices, this easy recipe is perfect for breakfast, brunch or even dinner. Add a green or orange vegetable, a slice of whole wheat bread and glass of milk to round up to 4 Choices.

1 SERVING: Calories 250; Fat 14g (Saturated 6g); Cholesterol 270mg; Sodium 310mg; Carbohydrate 21g (Dietary Fiber 2g); Protein 12g **Food Exchanges:** 1 Starch; 1 High-Fat Meat; 1 Vegetable; 1 Fat

Stuffed French Toast

Prep Time: 15 Minutes **Start to Finish:** 20 Minutes **6 servings**

2½
Carbohydrate
Choices

12 slices French bread, ½ inch thick
6 tablespoons fat-free soft cream cheese
¼ cup preserves or jam (any flavor)
4 egg whites, 2 eggs or ½ cup fat-free cholesterol-free egg product, slightly beaten
½ cup fat-free (skim) milk
2 tablespoons sugar

1 Spread one side of 6 slices bread with 1 tablespoon of the cream cheese. Spread one side of remaining slices with 2 teaspoons of the preserves. Place bread with cream cheese and bread with preserves together in pairs.

2 Beat egg whites, milk and sugar with wire whisk until smooth; pour into shallow bowl.

3 Spray griddle or skillet with cooking spray; heat griddle to 325°F or heat skillet over medium-low heat. Dip each side of sandwich into egg mixture. Cook sandwiches 2 to 3 minutes on each side or until golden brown.

Note from Dr. B Breakfast eaters usually eat better overall than those who skip—it's so important to fuel up first thing in the morning. Even when you're in a hurry, take time to grab a slice of toast, a carton of yogurt and a small piece of fruit on your way out the door.

2 SLICES: Calories 205; Fat 2g (Saturated 0g); Cholesterol 0mg; Sodium 410mg; Carbohydrate 40g (Dietary Fiber 2g); Protein 9g **Food Exchanges:** 2 Starch; ½ Skim Milk

Oatmeal Pancakes with Maple-Cranberry Syrup

Prep Time: 10 Minutes   **Start to Finish:** 25 Minutes   **12 servings**

Maple-Cranberry Syrup
½ cup artificially sweetened maple-flavored syrup
¼ cup whole berry cranberry sauce

Oatmeal Pancakes
½ cup quick-cooking or old-fashioned oats
¼ cup all-purpose flour
¼ cup whole wheat flour
¾ cup buttermilk
¼ cup fat-free (skim) milk
1 tablespoon sugar
2 tablespoons canola or vegetable oil
1 teaspoon baking powder
½ teaspoon baking soda
½ teaspoon salt
1 egg or ¼ cup fat-free cholesterol-free egg product

1 Heat syrup ingredients in 1-quart saucepan over medium heat, stirring occasionally, until cranberry sauce is melted. Keep warm. Beat pancake ingredients with hand beater or wire whisk just until smooth. (For thinner pancakes, stir in additional 2 to 4 tablespoons milk.)

2 Spray griddle or 10-inch nonstick skillet with cooking spray; heat griddle to 375°F or heat skillet over medium heat. For each pancake, pour slightly less than ¼ cup batter from cup or pitcher onto hot griddle.

3 Cook pancakes until puffed and dry around edges. Turn; cook other sides until golden brown. Serve with syrup.

Note from Dr. B Oatmeal is 100 percent whole grain; using it in baked goods adds fiber and texture. Recent studies have revealed that eating 1 cup of cooked oatmeal two to four times per week has been linked to a reduction in risk for type 2 diabetes.

1 PANCAKE WITH SYRUP: Calories 170; Fat 7g (Saturated 1g); Cholesterol 35mg; Sodium 480mg; Carbohydrate 23g (Dietary Fiber 1g); Protein 5g **Food Exchanges:** 1½ Starch; ½ Fat

Fruit Parfaits

Prep Time: 10 Minutes **Start to Finish:** 10 Minutes **2 servings**

2 Carbohydrate Choices

½ cup chopped cantaloupe
½ cup sliced strawberries
½ cup sliced kiwifruit or honeydew melon
½ banana, sliced
1 cup vanilla artificially sweetened low-fat yogurt
2 tablespoons sliced almonds, toasted*

1 Alternate layers of fruit and yogurt in 2 goblets or parfait glasses, beginning and ending with fruit.

2 Top with almonds.

*To toast nuts, bake uncovered in ungreased shallow pan in 350°F oven about 10 minutes, stirring occasionally, until golden brown. Or cook in ungreased heavy skillet over medium-low heat 5 to 7 minutes, stirring frequently until browning begins, then stirring constantly until golden brown.

Betty's Success Tip This tasty fruit and yogurt combination has all the calories and carbohydrates you need for a hearty breakfast. It also makes a great lunch or between-meal snack.

1 SERVING: Calories 160; Fat 5g (Saturated 1g); Cholesterol 0mg; Sodium 60mg; Carbohydrate 26g (Dietary Fiber 5g); Protein 8g **Food Exchanges:** 1½ Fruit; ½ Skim Milk

SMART SNACKS
AND BREADS

Roasted Vegetable Dip

1/2
Carbohydrate
Choices

Prep Time: 15 Minutes   **Start to Finish:** 45 Minutes   **7 servings (¼ cup each)**

1 medium zucchini, sliced (2 cups)
1 medium yellow summer squash, sliced (1½ cups)
1 medium red bell pepper, sliced
1 medium red onion, thinly sliced
2 cloves garlic, peeled
Cooking spray
½ teaspoon salt
¼ teaspoon ground red pepper (cayenne)
Dippers, if desired

1 Heat oven to 400°F. Spread zucchini, yellow squash, bell pepper, onion and garlic in 15 × 10 × 1-inch jelly roll pan. Spray vegetables with cooking spray. Sprinkle with salt and red pepper.

2 Bake about 30 minutes, turning vegetables once, until vegetables are tender and lightly browned.

3 Place vegetables in blender or food processor. Cover and blend on high speed about 1 minute, stopping blender occasionally to scrape sides, until smooth.

4 Serve warm, or refrigerate at least 2 hours until chilled. Serve with dippers.

Betty's Success Tip Dips, especially healthy ones like this, along with plenty of fun dippers make great excuses for getting together. Try dipping baby-cut carrots, cucumber slices, green bell pepper strips, toasted pita bread wedges or baked tortilla chips.

1 SERVING: Calories 20; Fat 0g (Saturated 0g); Cholesterol 0mg; Sodium 170mg; Carbohydrate 5g (Dietary Fiber 1g); Protein 1g **Food Exchanges:** ½ Starch; 1 Vegetable

Veggies and Cheese Mini-Pizzas

Prep Time: 10 Minutes **Start to Finish:** 15 Minutes **4 servings**

2 pita breads (6 inches in diameter)
4 roma (plum) tomatoes, chopped (1 cup)
2 small zucchini, chopped (2 cups)
1 small onion, chopped (¼ cup)
2 tablespoons sliced ripe olives
1 teaspoon chopped fresh or ¼ teaspoon dried basil leaves
¼ cup spaghetti sauce or pizza sauce
¾ cup shredded mozzarella cheese (3 ounces)

1 Heat oven to 425°F. Split each pita bread around edge with knife to make 2 rounds. Place rounds on ungreased cookie sheet. Bake about 5 minutes or just until crisp.

2 Mix tomatoes, zucchini, onion, olives and basil. Spread spaghetti sauce evenly over rounds. Top with vegetable mixture. Sprinkle with cheese.

3 Bake 5 to 7 minutes or until cheese is melted. Cut into wedges.

Note from Dr. B Vegetables are loaded with the nutrients you need each day to be healthy. The Diabetes Food Guide Pyramid recommends three to five servings of veggies every day.

1 SERVING: Calories 170; Fat 5g (Saturated 3g); Cholesterol 10mg; Sodium 370mg; Carbohydrate 24g (Dietary Fiber 3g); Protein 10g **Food Exchanges:** 1 Starch; 2 Vegetable; 1 Fat

See photo on page 33.

Chewy Pizza Bread

Prep Time: 10 Minutes   **Start to Finish:** 30 Minutes   **8 servings (2 squares each)**

1½
Carbohydrate
Choices

1½ cups all-purpose flour
1½ teaspoons baking powder
½ teaspoon salt
¾ cup regular or nonalcoholic beer
½ cup spaghetti sauce
⅓ cup shredded low-fat mozzarella cheese
Chopped fresh basil leaves, if desired

1 Heat oven to 425°F. Spray square pan, 8 × 8 × 2 inches, with cooking spray. Mix flour, baking powder and salt in medium bowl. Stir in beer just until flour is moistened. Spread dough in pan. Spread spaghetti sauce over dough. Sprinkle with cheese.

2 Bake 15 to 20 minutes or until toothpick inserted in center comes out clean. Sprinkle with basil. Cut into 2-inch squares. Serve warm.

Betty's Success Tip This bread also makes a great dipper for pizza or pasta sauce. Instead of cutting into squares, just slice into long, thin "fingers" that are easier to dip. Pass individual small bowls of sauce to make dipping easier.

1 SERVING: Calories 130; Fat 2g (Saturated 1g); Cholesterol 5mg; Sodium 340mg; Carbohydrate 24g (Dietary Fiber 1g); Protein 4g **Food Exchanges:** 1½ Starch

Crunchy Chicken Chunks with Thai Peanut Sauce

Prep Time: 10 Minutes **Start to Finish:** 35 Minutes **8 servings**

Crunchy Chicken Chunks
1½ cups cornflakes cereal, crushed (½ cup)
½ cup Original Bisquick® mix
¾ teaspoon paprika
¼ teaspoon salt
¼ teaspoon pepper
1 pound boneless, skinless chicken breasts, cut into 1-inch pieces
Cooking spray

Thai Peanut Sauce
½ cup plain low-fat yogurt
¼ cup creamy peanut butter
½ cup fat-free (skim) milk
1 tablespoon soy sauce
⅛ teaspoon ground red pepper (cayenne), if desired

1 Heat oven to 400°F. Line jelly roll pan, 15 × 10 × 1 inch, with aluminum foil.

2 Mix cereal, Bisquick mix, paprika, salt and pepper in 2-quart resealable plastic food-storage bag. Shake about 6 chicken pieces at a time in bag until coated. Shake off any extra crumbs. Place chicken pieces in pan. Spray with cooking spray.

3 Bake uncovered 20 to 25 minutes or until coating is crisp and chicken is no longer pink in center.

4 Mix all sauce ingredients in 10-inch nonstick skillet. Cook over medium heat 3 to 4 minutes, stirring occasionally, until mixture begins to thicken. Serve sauce with chicken.

Note from Dr. B Rich in vitamins, minerals and heart-healthy fat, peanut butter, enjoyed in moderation, provides satisfaction. A modest amount may prevent you from over-indulging on other foods.

1 SERVING: Calories 180; Fat 7g (Saturated 2g); Cholesterol 35mg; Sodium 440mg; Carbohydrate 13g (Dietary Fiber 0g); Protein 17g **Food Exchanges:** 1 Starch; 2 Lean Meat

Crunchy Chicken Chunks with Thai Peanut Sauce
and Veggies and Cheese Mini-Pizzas (page 30)

Cinnamon–Raisin Snack Mix

Prep Time: 5 Minutes **Start to Finish:** 10 Minutes **10 servings (½ cup each)**

2
Carbohydrate
Choices

¼ cup sugar
1 teaspoon ground cinnamon
¼ cup butter or margarine
1½ cups Corn Chex® cereal
1½ cups Rice Chex® cereal
1½ cups Wheat Chex® cereal
½ cup raisins, dried cranberries or dried cherries

1 Mix sugar and cinnamon; set aside.

2 Place butter in large microwavable bowl. Microwave uncovered on High about 40 seconds or until melted. Stir in cereals until evenly coated. Microwave uncovered 2 minutes, stirring after 1 minute.

3 Sprinkle half of the sugar mixture evenly over cereals; stir. Sprinkle with remaining sugar mixture; stir. Microwave uncovered 1 minute. Stir in raisins. Spread on paper towels to cool.

Betty's Success Tip Cereals give you a lot of bang for your buck. Because cereals are fortified, cereal snacks are high in iron and other vitamins and minerals. As long as you keep track of the serving amount and watch your total carbohydrate level, you can snack away on them!

1 SERVING: Calories 155; Fat 5g (Saturated 3g); Cholesterol 10mg; Sodium 190mg; Carbohydrate 27g (Dietary Fiber 1g); Protein 2g **Food Exchanges:** 1 Starch; 1 Fruit; 1 Fat

Parmesan–Herb Breadsticks

Prep Time: 15 Minutes **Start to Finish:** 1 Hour **12 breadsticks**

1
Carbohydrate
Choices

Olive oil
Cornmeal, if desired
12 frozen whole wheat or white bread dough rolls (from 48-ounce package), thawed
2 tablespoons olive or canola oil
3 or 4 long fresh rosemary sprigs
1 tablespoon grated Parmesan cheese

1 Brush 2 cookie sheets with olive oil; sprinkle with cornmeal. Roll each ball of dough into 9-inch rope. Place ropes about ½-inch apart on cookie sheets.

2 Brush 2 tablespoons oil over dough. Break 36 small clusters of rosemary leaves off rosemary sprigs. Using 3 clusters for each breadstick, insert stem end of each cluster ¼ inch deep into top of breadstick. Sprinkle cheese over dough. Cover loosely with plastic wrap and let rise in warm place about 30 minutes or until almost double.

3 Heat oven to 350°F. Bake 12 to 15 minutes or until light golden brown. Serve warm.

Betty's Success Tip A great snack by itself or with any of the soups in Chapter 6, these whole wheat and herb breadsticks can be dipped into pasta or cheese sauce. Just check the label for number of carbohydrates and convert that to Choices, using the "How Many Carbohydrate Choices?" conversion guide on page 10.

1 BREADSTICK: Calories 120; Fat 5g (Saturated 1g); Cholesterol 0mg; Sodium 200mg; Carbohydrate 17g (Dietary Fiber 2g); Protein 4g **Food Exchanges:** 1 Starch; 1 Fat

See photo on page 69.

Cheddar and Green Onion Biscuits

Prep Time: 15 Minutes **Start to Finish:** 25 Minutes **8 biscuits**

1⅓ cups all-purpose flour
1½ teaspoons baking powder
½ teaspoon salt
¼ teaspoon baking soda
¼ teaspoon ground mustard
4 medium green onions, sliced (¼ cup)
½ cup shredded reduced-fat Cheddar cheese (2 ounces)
¾ cup buttermilk
3 tablespoons canola or vegetable oil

1 Heat oven to 450°F. Spray cookie sheet with cooking spray. Mix flour, baking powder, salt, baking soda and mustard in medium bowl. Stir in onions and cheese.

2 Mix buttermilk and oil; stir into flour mixture until soft dough forms. Drop dough by 8 spoonfuls onto cookie sheet.

3 Bake 9 to 11 minutes or until golden brown. Serve warm.

Betty's Success Tip You wouldn't know it by the name, but buttermilk contains no butter and has very little fat. Buttermilk is a calcium-rich, refreshing beverage. It also adds tang and a wonderful dairy flavor to salad dressings, dips and baked goods.

1 BISCUIT: Calories 140; Fat 6g (Saturated 1g); Cholesterol 5mg; Sodium 340mg; Carbohydrate 18g (Dietary Fiber12g); Protein 5g **Food Exchanges:** 1 Starch; 1 Fat

See photo on page 47.

FAMILY-PLEASING POULTRY AND FISH

Easy Mexican Chicken and Beans

Prep Time: 10 Minutes **Start to Finish:** 30 Minutes **4 servings**

1 pound boneless, skinless chicken breast strips for stir-fry
1 envelope (1.25 ounces) taco seasoning mix
1 can (15 to 16 ounces) black or pinto beans, rinsed and drained
1 can (11 ounces) whole kernel corn with red and green peppers, undrained
¼ cup water

1 Spray 10-inch nonstick skillet with cooking spray. Cook chicken in skillet over medium-high heat 8 to 10 minutes, stirring occasionally, until no longer pink in center.

2 Stir in seasoning mix, beans, corn and water. Cook over medium-high heat 8 to 10 minutes, stirring frequently, until sauce is slightly thickened. Serve with tortillas.

Note from Dr. B Boost your fiber with beans. Filled with many other important nutrients, beans are an excellent source of fiber that's so important for good blood glucose management and to keep your digestive tract moving.

1 SERVING: Calories 335; Fat 5g (Saturated 0g); Cholesterol 70mg; Sodium 780mg; Carbohydrate 48g (Dietary Fiber 12g); Protein 37g **Food Exchanges:** 2½ Starch; 4 Very Lean Meat

Baked Chicken and Rice with Autumn Vegetables

Prep Time: 20 Minutes   **Start to Finish:** 50 Minutes   **5 servings**

1 package (about 6 ounces) chicken-flavored rice mix or 1 package (6.9 ounces)
chicken-flavored rice and vermicelli mix
2 cups 1-inch pieces butternut squash
1 medium zucchini, cut lengthwise in half, then crosswise into ¾-inch slices
1 medium red bell pepper, cut into 1-inch pieces (1 cup)
4 boneless, skinless chicken breast (about 1¼ pounds)
2 cups water
½ cup garlic-and-herb spreadable cheese

1 Heat oven to 425°F. Mix rice, contents of seasoning packet, squash, zucchini and bell pepper in ungreased rectangular pan, 13 × 9 × 2 inches.

2 Spray 10-inch skillet with cooking spray; heat over medium-high heat. Cook chicken in skillet about 5 minutes, turning once, until brown. Remove chicken from skillet.

3 Add water to skillet; heat to boiling. Pour boiling water over rice mixture; stir to mix. Stir in cheese. Place chicken on rice mixture.

4 Cover and bake about 30 minutes or until liquid is absorbed and juice of chicken is clear when center of thickest part is cut (170°F).

Note from Dr. B Just 1 serving of this chicken and rice with vegetables gives you all the vitamin A and half of the vitamin C you need for the day. The secret ingredients? Butternut squash and red bell peppers!

1 SERVING: Calories 240; Fat 7g (Saturated 3g); Cholesterol 70mg; Sodium 360mg; Carbohydrate 19g (Dietary Fiber 2g); Protein 27g **Food Exchanges:** 1 Starch; 3 Lean Meat; 1 Vegetable

Parmesan-Dijon Chicken

1/2
Carbohydrate
Choices

Prep Time: 5 Minutes   **Start to Finish:** 30 Minutes   **6 servings**

¾ cup dry bread crumbs
¼ cup grated Parmesan cheese
¼ cup canola oil or butter, melted
2 tablespoons Dijon mustard
6 boneless, skinless chicken breast (about 1¾ pounds)

1 Heat oven to 375°F. Grease bottom and sides of rectangular pan, 13 × 9 × 2 inches, with shortening.

2 Mix bread crumbs and cheese in large resealable plastic food-storage bag. Mix oil and mustard in shallow dish. Dip chicken into oil mixture, then shake in bag to coat with crumb mixture. Place in pan.

3 Bake uncovered 20 to 25 minutes, turning once, until juice of chicken is clear when center of thickest part is cut (170°F).

Note from Dr. B To reduce fat and calories, trim all visible fat from meat and remove chicken skin before cooking.

1 SERVING: Calories 285; Fat 14g (Saturated 3g); Cholesterol 7mg; Sodium 440mg; Carbohydrate 10g (Dietary Fiber 0g); Protein 30g **Food Exchanges:** ½ Starch; 4 Lean Meat

See photo on page 56.

Lemony Fish over Vegetables and Rice

Prep Time: 10 Minutes **Start to Finish:** 25 Minutes **4 servings**

1 package (6.2 ounces) fried rice (rice and vermicelli mix with almonds and
    Oriental seasonings)
2 tablespoons butter or margarine
2 cups water
½ teaspoon grated lemon peel
1 bag (1 pound) frozen corn, broccoli and red peppers (or other combination)
1 pound mild-flavored fish fillets (such as cod, flounder, sole or walleye pike),
    about ½ inch thick
½ teaspoon lemon pepper
1 tablespoon lemon juice
2 tablespoons chopped fresh parsley

1 Cook rice and butter in 12-inch nonstick skillet over medium heat 2 to
3 minutes, stirring occasionally, until rice is golden brown. Stir in water,
seasoning packet from rice mix and lemon peel. Heat to boiling; reduce
heat. Cover and simmer 10 minutes.

2 Stir in frozen vegetables. Heat to boiling, stirring occasionally. Cut fish into
4 serving pieces; arrange on rice mixture. Sprinkle fish with lemon pepper;
drizzle with lemon juice. Reduce heat.

3 Cover and simmer 8 to 10 minutes or until fish flakes easily with fork and
vegetables are tender. Sprinkle with parsley.

Betty's Success Tip This simple one-pan recipe is a huge help when you
need to prepare dinner in a flash. If you would rather use another vegetable
combination, select one you prefer and prepare the dish the same way.

1 SERVING: Calories 230; Fat 7g (Saturated 1g); Cholesterol 55mg; Sodium 330mg; Carbohydrate 22g (Dietary
Fiber 3g); Protein 23g **Food Exchanges:** 1 Starch; 2½ Lean Meat; 1 Vegetable

Halibut with Lime and Cilantro

Prep Time: 10 Minutes **Start to Finish:** 45 Minutes **2 servings**

0
Carbohydrate
Choices

Lime-Cilantro Marinade
2 tablespoons lime juice
1 tablespoon chopped fresh cilantro
1 teaspoon olive or vegetable oil
1 clove garlic, finely chopped

Halibut
2 halibut or salmon steaks (about ¾ pound)
Freshly ground pepper to taste
½ cup salsa

1 Mix marinade ingredients in shallow glass or plastic dish or resealable plastic food-storage bag. Add fish; turn several times to coat with marinade. Cover and refrigerate 15 minutes, turning once.

2 Heat coals or gas grill for direct heat. Remove fish from marinade; discard marinade. Cover and grill fish 4 to 6 inches from medium heat 10 to 20 minutes, turning once, until fish flakes easily with fork. Sprinkle with pepper. Serve with salsa.

Note from Dr. B Be sure to take your medications as prescribed. If you have any questions, ask your doctor or pharmacist. Know when to take them, with what, how to store them and how to avoid side effects. Take a list of all your medications, the doses and how often you take them to each doctor visit.

1 SERVING: Calories 150; Fat 3g (Saturated 1g); Cholesterol 75mg; Sodium 400mg; Carbohydrate 5g (Dietary Fiber 1g); Protein 27g **Food Exchanges:** 3½ Very Lean Meat; 1 Vegetable

Halibut with Lime and Cilantro and Bulgur Pilaf (page 60)

Italian Shrimp Stir-Fry

3 Carbohydrate Choices

Prep Time: 15 Minutes   **Start to Finish:** 30 Minutes   **5 servings**

8 ounces uncooked linguine
¾ cup reduced-calorie Italian dressing
1½ teaspoons grated lemon peel
3 cloves garlic, finely chopped
¾ pound fresh or frozen (thawed) uncooked medium shrimp, peeled and deveined
3 cups broccoli flowerets
1 medium yellow summer squash, cut lengthwise in half, then cut crosswise into slices
      (1½ cups)
2 tablespoons water
8 cherry tomatoes, cut in half
12 extra-large pitted ripe olives, cut in half
¼ cup chopped fresh basil leaves
Grated Parmesan cheese, if desired

1 Cook and drain linguine as directed on package; keep warm. Mix dressing, lemon peel and garlic; set aside.

2 Spray 12-inch nonstick skillet with cooking spray; heat over medium-high heat. Add shrimp; stir-fry about 2 minutes or until shrimp are pink. Remove shrimp from skillet.

3 Spray skillet with cooking spray; heat over medium-high heat. Add broccoli and squash; stir-fry 1 minute. Add water. Cover and simmer about 3 minutes, stirring occasionally, until vegetables are crisp-tender (add water if necessary to prevent sticking).

4 Stir in dressing mixture; cook 30 seconds. Stir in tomatoes, olives, basil, shrimp and linguine; stir-fry until hot. Sprinkle with cheese.

Betty's Success Tip This quick and easy stir-fry was a real winner in our test kitchens. If you prefer chicken to shrimp, use ¾ pound boneless, skinless chicken breasts, cut into 1-inch pieces. Stir-fry the chicken 3 to 4 minutes or until no longer pink in the center.

1 SERVING: Calories 310; Fat 3g (Saturated 1g); Cholesterol 100mg; Sodium 660mg; Carbohydrate 45g (Dietary Fiber 4g); Protein 19g **Food Exchanges:** 2 Starch; 1 Medium-Fat Meat; 3 Vegetable

Italian Shrimp Stir-Fry and Cheddar
and Green Onion Biscuits (page 37)

Marvelous Meat

Orange Teriyaki Beef with Noodles

1½ Carbohydrate Choices

Prep Time: 5 Minutes   **Start to Finish:** 20 Minutes   **4 servings**

1 pound beef boneless sirloin, cut into thin strips
1 can (14 ounces) beef broth
¼ cup teriyaki stir-fry sauce
2 tablespoons orange marmalade
Dash of ground red pepper (cayenne)
1½ cups snap pea pods
1½ cups uncooked fine egg noodles (3 ounces)

1 Spray 12-inch skillet with cooking spray; heat over medium-high heat. Cook beef in skillet 2 to 4 minutes, stirring occasionally, until brown. Remove beef from skillet; keep warm.

2 Add broth, stir-fry sauce, marmalade and red pepper to skillet. Heat to boiling. Stir in pea pods and noodles; reduce heat to medium. Cover and cook about 5 minutes or until noodles are tender.

3 Stir in beef. Cook uncovered 2 to 3 minutes or until sauce is slightly thickened.

Betty's Success Tip Garnish this dish with orange slices and chopped fresh chives. If you want to add a great salad, take a bag of prewashed spinach and toss with mandarin orange segments. Top with raspberry vinaigrette or fat-free sweet-and-sour dressing and chopped green onions.

1 SERVING: Calories 230; Fat 4g (Saturated 1g); Cholesterol 75mg; Sodium 1210mg; Carbohydrate 21g (Dietary Fiber 1g); Protein 28g **Food Exchanges:** 1 Starch; 3 Very Lean Meat; 1 Vegetable

Beef, Lettuce and Tomato Wraps

1½
Carbohydrate
Choices

Prep Time: 20 Minutes   **Start to Finish:** 30 Minutes   **4 servings**

1½ tablespoons chili powder
2 teaspoons dried oregano leaves
1 teaspoon ground cumin
1 teaspoon salt
1 pound beef top sirloin steak, about ¾-inch thick
4 flour tortillas (6 to 8 inches in diameter)
¾ cup reduced-fat sour cream
1 tablespoon prepared horseradish
4 cups shredded lettuce
1 large tomato, chopped (1 cup)

1 Mix chili powder, oregano, cumin and salt. Rub mixture on both sides of beef. Let stand 10 minutes at room temperature.

2 Set oven control to broil. Place beef on rack in broiler pan. Broil with top 3 to 4 inches from heat about 5 minutes on each side for medium doneness or until beef is of desired doneness. Cut into ⅛-inch slices.

3 Warm tortillas as directed on package. Mix sour cream and horseradish. Spread 3 tablespoons horseradish mixture over each tortilla; top each with 1 cup of the lettuce and ¼ cup of the tomato. Top with beef. Wrap tortillas around filling.

Note from Dr. B Broiling, braising and roasting are healthy, low-fat techniques to use when preparing meats. Grilling also allows the fat to drip away from the meat.

1 SERVING: Calories 280; Fat 9g (Saturated 4g); Cholesterol 75mg; Sodium 820mg; Carbohydrate 24g (Dietary Fiber 3g); Protein 29g   **Food Exchanges:** 1½ Starch; 4 Lean Meat

Pork Tenderloin with Roasted Vegetables

2
Carbohydrate Choices

Prep Time: 10 Minutes   **Start to Finish:** 55 Minutes   **6 servings**

2 pork tenderloins (each about ¾ pound)
1 pound baby-cut carrots
2 pounds new potatoes (16 to 20), cut in half
1 medium onion, cut into wedges
6 whole cloves garlic
1 tablespoon olive or canola oil
2 teaspoons dried rosemary leaves, crumbled
1 teaspoon dried sage leaves, crumbled
¼ teaspoon salt
¼ teaspoon pepper

1 Heat oven to 450°F. Spray shallow roasting pan with cooking spray. Place pork in pan. Insert meat thermometer so tip is in thickest part of pork. Place carrots, potatoes, onion and garlic around pork. Drizzle with oil; sprinkle with rosemary, sage, salt and pepper.

2 Bake uncovered 25 to 30 minutes or until thermometer reads 155°F. Remove pork from pan. Stir vegetables and continue baking 5 to 10 minutes or until tender. Cover pork and let stand 10 to 15 minutes or until pork has slight blush of pink in center and meat thermometer reads 160°F. Serve pork with vegetables and garlic.

Betty's Success Tip Here's a dish that's elegant enough for company and still fits your meal plan. Even better, it all bakes in one pan for easy cleanup!

1 SERVING: Calories 310; Fat 6g (Saturated 2g); Cholesterol 70mg; Sodium 190mg; Carbohydrate 41g (Dietary Fiber 6g); Protein 29g **Food Exchanges:** 2 Starch; 3 Very Lean Meat; 1 Vegetable

Couscous and Sweet Potatoes with Pork

Prep Time: 10 Minutes   **Start to Finish:** 20 Minutes   **5 servings**

1¼ cups uncooked couscous
1 pound pork tenderloin, thinly sliced
1 medium sweet potato, peeled and cut into julienne strips
1 cup thick-and-chunky salsa
½ cup water
2 tablespoons honey
¼ cup chopped fresh cilantro

1 Cook couscous as directed on package.

2 While couscous is cooking, spray 12-inch skillet with cooking spray. Cook pork in skillet over medium heat 2 to 3 minutes, stirring occasionally, until no longer pink in center.

3 Stir sweet potato, salsa, water and honey into pork. Heat to boiling; reduce heat to medium. Cover and cook 5 to 6 minutes, stirring occasionally, until potato is tender. Sprinkle with cilantro. Serve pork mixture over couscous.

Betty's Success Tip Want a little crunch with this quick pasta and pork dinner? Try baby-cut carrots, apple wedges, bell pepper strips or celery sticks.

1 SERVING: Calories 325; Fat 4g (Saturated 1g); Cholesterol 55mg; Sodium 270mg; Carbohydrate 49g (Dietary Fiber 4g); Protein 27g **Food Exchanges:** 3 Starch; 2 Very Lean Meat; 1 Vegetable

Breaded Pork Chops

Prep Time: 10 Minutes **Start to Finish:** 20 Minutes **8 servings**

½ cup Original Bisquick mix
12 saltine crackers, crushed (½ cup)
1 teaspoon seasoned salt
¼ teaspoon pepper
1 egg or ¼ cup fat-free cholesterol-free egg product
2 tablespoons water
8 pork boneless loin chops, ½ inch thick (about 2 pounds)

1 Mix Bisquick, cracker crumbs, seasoned salt and pepper. Mix egg and water.

2 Dip pork into egg mixture, then coat with Bisquick mixture.

3 Spray 12-inch nonstick skillet with cooking spray; heat over medium-high heat. Cook pork in skillet 8 to 10 minutes, turning once, until no longer pink in center.

Betty's Success Tip Breading for fish, chicken, meat or vegetables doesn't have to be heavy. This one combines Bisquick, crackers and seasonings for a flavorful, low-carbohydrate option.

1 SERVING: Calories 215; Fat 10g (Saturated 3g); Cholesterol 90mg; Sodium 370mg; Carbohydrate 8g (Dietary Fiber 0g); Protein 24g **Food Exchanges:** ½ Starch; 3 Lean Meat

See photo on page 79.

GREAT GRAINS,
LEGUMES AND PASTA

Barley and Asparagus and
Parmesan-Dijon Chicken (page 42)

Barley and Asparagus

Prep Time: 15 Minutes **Start to Finish:** 45 Minutes **8 servings (½ cup each)**

2 tablespoons canola oil or butter
1 medium onion, chopped (½ cup)
1 medium carrot, chopped (½ cup)
1 cup uncooked quick-cooking barley
2 cans (14 ounces each) chicken broth, heated
8 ounces asparagus (8 to 10 stalks), cut into 1-inch pieces
2 tablespoons shredded Parmesan cheese
¼ teaspoon dried marjoram or thyme leaves
⅛ teaspoon pepper

1 Heat oil in 12-inch skillet over medium heat. Cook onion and carrot in oil 1 to 2 minutes, stirring occasionally, until crisp-tender. Stir in barley. Cook and stir 1 minute.

2 Pour 1 cup of the hot broth over barley mixture. Cook un-covered about 5 minutes, stirring occasionally, until liquid is absorbed. Stir in asparagus. Continue cooking 15 to 20 minutes, adding broth 1 cup at a time and stirring frequently, until barley is tender and liquid is absorbed; remove from heat. Stir in remaining ingredients.

Betty's Success Tip Cooking grains in chicken, beef or vegetable broth adds to the overall flavor of the dish. You can also cook grains like barley, rice, quinoa or bulgur in apple juice or eight-vegetable juice for extra flavor.

1 SERVING: Calories 130; Fat 4g (Saturated 2g); Cholesterol 10mg; Sodium 520mg; Carbohydrate 23g (Dietary Fiber 5g); Protein 6g **Food Exchanges:** 1 Starch; 1 Vegetable; ½ Fat

Creamy Quinoa Primavera

Prep Time: 5 Minutes   **Start to Finish:** 30 Minutes   **6 servings**

2
Carbohydrate
Choices

1½ cups uncooked quinoa

3 cups chicken broth

1 package (3 ounces) cream cheese

1 tablespoon chopped fresh or 1 teaspoon dried basil leaves

2 teaspoons canola oil or butter

2 cloves garlic, finely chopped

5 cups thinly sliced or bite-size pieces assorted vegetables (such as asparagus, broccoli, carrot, zucchini)

2 tablespoons grated Romano cheese

1 Rinse quinoa thoroughly; drain. Heat quinoa and broth to boiling in 2-quart saucepan; reduce heat. Cover and simmer 10 to 15 minutes or until all broth is absorbed. Stir in cream cheese and basil.

2 Heat oil in 10-inch nonstick skillet over medium-high heat. Cook garlic in oil about 30 seconds, stirring frequently, until golden. Stir in vegetables. Cook about 5 minutes, stirring frequently, until vegetables are crisp-tender. Toss vegetables and quinoa mixture. Sprinkle with Romano cheese.

Note from Dr. B Regular, consistent exercise helps your body use insulin more effectively, all day and night. Physical activity also reduces the risk of heart attacks. Aim for a total of 30 to 60 minutes of moderate activity on most days. To reduce the risk of hypoglycemia (low blood glucose), exercise at the same time of day, each day.

1 SERVING: Calories 260; Fat 10g (Saturated 5g); Cholesterol 80mg; Sodium 630mg; Carbohydrate 36g (Dietary Fiber 5g); Protein 12g **Food Exchanges:** 2 Starch; ½ Medium-Fat Meat; 1 Vegetable; 1 Fat

Bulgur Pilaf

Prep Time: 15 Minutes   **Start to Finish:** 40 Minutes   **6 servings**

1
Carbohydrate
Choices

2 tablespoons canola oil or butter, melted
½ cup slivered almonds
1 medium onion, chopped (½ cup)
1 medium carrot, chopped (½ cup)
1 can (14 ounces) chicken broth
1 cup uncooked bulgur
¼ teaspoon lemon pepper seasoning salt or black pepper
¼ cup chopped fresh parsley

1 Heat 1 tablespoon of the oil in 12-inch skillet over medium-high heat. Cook almonds in oil 2 to 3 minutes, stirring constantly, until golden brown. Remove almonds from skillet.

2 Add remaining 1 tablespoon oil, the onion and carrot to skillet. Cook about 3 minutes, stirring occasionally, until vegetables are crisp-tender.

3 Stir in broth, bulgur and lemon pepper seasoning salt. Heat to boiling; reduce heat. Cover and simmer about 15 minutes or until bulgur is tender and liquid is absorbed. Stir in almonds and parsley.

Note from Dr. B Bulgur is made from wheat berries that have been partially cooked and cracked. Bulgur, a whole grain, imparts a nutty, whole wheat flavor with plenty of nutrients, such as phosphorus and iron.

1 SERVING: Calories 140; Fat 9g (Saturated 3g); Cholesterol 10mg; Sodium 630mg; Carbohydrate 13g (Dietary Fiber 4g); Protein 5g **Food Exchanges:** 1 Starch; 1½ Fat

See photo on page 45.

Vermicelli and Herbs

Prep Time: 10 Minutes   **Start to Finish:** 20 Minutes   **4 servings**

8 ounces uncooked vermicelli
2 tablespoons olive or canola oil
2 tablespoons chopped pine nuts
1 tablespoon chopped fresh parsley
1 tablespoon large capers, chopped
1 teaspoon chopped fresh rosemary leaves
1 teaspoon chopped fresh sage leaves
1 teaspoon chopped fresh basil leaves
1 cup cherry tomatoes, cut into fourths
Freshly ground pepper, if desired

1 Cook and drain vermicelli as directed on package.

2 Mix remaining ingredients except tomatoes and pepper in medium bowl. Stir in tomatoes. Toss vermicelli and herb mixture. Sprinkle with pepper.

Betty's Success Tip Herbs, especially fresh ones, impart an extra flavor boost to foods. To cut fat and calories, serve meatless meals at least once a week.

1 SERVING: Calories 290; Fat 11g (Saturated 1g); Cholesterol 0mg; Sodium 65mg; Carbohydrate 48g (Dietary Fiber 3g); Protein 9g **Food Exchanges:** 3 Starch; 2 Fat

Fettuccine with Asparagus and Mushrooms

1 Carbohydrate Choices

Prep Time: 10 Minutes   **Start to Finish:** 20 Minutes   **7 servings**

¼ cup sun-dried tomatoes (not in oil)

8 ounces uncooked fettuccine

1 teaspoon olive or canola oil

1 pound thin asparagus, broken into 2-inch pieces

1 pound mushrooms, sliced (6 cups)

2 cloves garlic, finely chopped

3 tablespoons chopped fresh parsley

2 tablespoons chopped fresh basil leaves

2 tablespoons cornstarch

½ teaspoon salt

¼ teaspoon pepper

1 cup dry white wine or chicken broth

1 cup chicken broth

¼ cup pine nuts

¼ cup freshly grated Parmesan cheese

1 Pour enough boiling water over dried tomatoes to cover. Let stand 10 minutes; drain. Chop tomatoes.

2 Cook and drain fettuccine as directed on package.

3 While fettuccine is cooking, heat oil in 12-inch skillet over medium heat. Cook asparagus, mushrooms, garlic, parsley and basil in oil 5 minutes, stirring occasionally. Stir in tomatoes. Simmer 2 to 3 minutes or until tomatoes are heated.

4 Beat cornstarch, salt and pepper into wine and broth in small bowl with wire whisk; stir into vegetable mixture. Heat to boiling over medium heat, stirring constantly, until mixture is smooth and bubbly; boil and stir 1 minute. Serve over fettuccine. Sprinkle with nuts and cheese.

Note from Dr. B This pasta dish is a bit lower in protein, so serve it with a slice of whole wheat bread and cheese. Or serve as a side dish to meat. You need to get enough protein every day to help build new cells and make antibodies to fight off infection.

1 SERVING: Calories 210; Fat 7g (Saturated 2g); Cholesterol 30mg; Sodium 580mg; Carbohydrate 30g (Dietary Fiber 3g); Protein 10g **Food Exchanges:** 1 Starch; 3 Vegetable; 1 Fat

White Bean and Spinach Pizza

Prep Time: 15 Minutes **Start to Finish:** 25 Minutes **6 servings**

2½
Carbohydrate
Choices

½ cup sun-dried tomato halves (not in oil)
1 can (15 to 16 ounces) great northern or navy beans, rinsed and drained
2 medium cloves garlic, finely chopped
1 package (10 ounces) ready-to-serve thin Italian pizza crust (12 inches in diameter)
¼ teaspoon dried oregano leaves
1 cup firmly packed spinach leaves, shredded
½ cup shredded reduced-fat Colby–Monterey Jack cheese (2 ounces)

1 Heat oven to 425°F. Pour enough boiling water over dried tomatoes to cover. Let stand 10 minutes; drain. Cut into thin strips; set aside.

2 Place beans and garlic in food processor. Cover and process until smooth.

3 Spread beans over pizza crust. Sprinkle with oregano, tomatoes, spinach and cheese. Place on ungreased cookie sheet. Bake about 10 minutes or until cheese is melted.

Betty's Success Tip When picking out your pizza crust, think thin. The thick-crust variety is much higher in carbohydrates, calories and fat per serving.

1 SERVING: Calories 233; Fat 2g (Saturated 1g); Cholesterol 50mg; Sodium 550mg; Carbohydrate 46g (Dietary Fiber 6g); Protein 15g **Food Exchanges:** 2 Starch; 1 Very Lean Meat; 2 Vegetable

SUSTAINING SOUPS AND STEWS

Southwest Chicken Soup with Baked Tortilla Strips

Prep Time: 15 Minutes   **Start to Finish:** 7 Hours 45 Minutes   **6 servings**

Southwest Chicken Soup

1 pound boneless, skinless chicken thighs, cut into 1-inch pieces
2 medium sweet potatoes, peeled and cut into 1-inch pieces (2 cups)
1 large onion, chopped (1 cup)
2 cans (14.5 ounces each) diced tomatoes with green chilies, undrained
1 can (14 ounces) chicken broth
1 teaspoon dried oregano leaves
½ teaspoon ground cumin
1 cup frozen whole kernel corn
½ cup chopped green bell pepper
2 tablespoons chopped fresh cilantro

Baked Tortilla Strips

8 yellow or blue corn tortillas (5 or 6 inches in diameter)

1 Mix chicken, sweet potatoes, onion, tomatoes, broth, oregano and cumin in 3½- to 4-quart slow cooker.

2 Cover and cook on Low heat setting 7 to 8 hours. Stir in corn and bell pepper. Cover and cook on High heat setting about 30 minutes or until chicken is no longer pink in center and vegetables are tender.

3 Meanwhile, make tortilla strips. Heat oven to 450°F. Spray 2 cookie sheets with cooking spray. Cut each tortilla into strips. Place in single layer on cookie sheets. Bake about 6 minutes or until crisp but not brown; cool.

4 Spoon soup into individual bowls. Top with tortilla strips. Sprinkle with cilantro.

Note from Dr. B Sweet potatoes, squash, carrots and other bright orange vegetables contain beta-carotene, which your body converts to vitamin A. It's vital for proper eyesight and healthy hair and skin.

1 SERVING: Calories 295; Fat 7g (Saturated 2g); Cholesterol 45mg; Sodium 770mg; Carbohydrate 41g (Dietary Fiber 5g); Protein 22g **Food Exchanges:** 2 Starch; 2 Lean Meat; 1 Vegetable

Beef-Barley Stew

Prep Time: 15 Minutes **Start to Finish:** 1 Hour 25 Minutes **6 servings**

1½
Carbohydrate
Choices

1 pound extra-lean ground beef
1 medium onion, chopped (½ cup)
2 cups beef broth
⅔ cup uncooked barley
2 teaspoons chopped fresh or ½ teaspoon dried oregano leaves
¼ teaspoon salt
¼ teaspoon pepper
1 can (14.5 ounces) whole tomatoes, undrained
1 can (8 ounces) sliced water chestnuts, undrained
1 package (10 ounces) frozen mixed vegetables

1 Heat oven to 350°F. Spray 10-inch nonstick skillet with cooking spray. Cook beef and onion in skillet over medium heat 7 to 8 minutes, stirring occasionally, until beef is brown; drain.

2 Mix beef mixture and remaining ingredients except frozen vegetables in ungreased 3-quart casserole, breaking up tomatoes.

3 Cover and bake 30 minutes. Stir in frozen vegetables. Cover and bake 30 to 40 minutes longer or until barley is tender.

Note from Dr. B One cup of cooked barley packs about 6 grams of fiber. This virtually fat-free whole grain also contains complex carbohydrates, B vitamins and protein.

1 SERVING: Calories 250; Fat 9g (Saturated 3g); Cholesterol 45mg; Sodium 600mg; Carbohydrate 29g (Dietary Fiber 6g); Protein 20g **Food Exchanges:** 1 Starch; 2 Lean Meat; 2 Vegetable

Beef-Barley Stew and
Parmesan-Herb Breadsticks (page 36)

Asian Pork and Noodle Soup

Prep Time: 10 Minutes **Start to Finish:** 30 Minutes **5 servings**

1
Carbohydrate
Choices

1 pound pork boneless sirloin or loin, cut into ½-inch pieces
2 cloves garlic, finely chopped
2 teaspoons finely chopped gingerroot
2 cans (14 ounces each) chicken broth
2 cups water
2 tablespoons soy sauce
2 cups uncooked fine egg noodles (4 ounces)
1 medium carrot, sliced (½ cup)
1 small red bell pepper, chopped (½ cup)
2 cups fresh spinach leaves

1 Spray 3-quart saucepan with cooking spray; heat over medium-high heat. Add pork, garlic and gingerroot; stir-fry 3 to 5 minutes or until pork is brown.

2 Stir in broth, water and soy sauce. Heat to boiling; reduce heat. Simmer uncovered 5 minutes. Stir in noodles, carrot and bell pepper. Simmer uncovered about 10 minutes or until noodles are tender.

3 Stir in spinach; cook until heated through.

Note from Dr. B For only 1 Carbohydrate Choice, this soup is nutrient-dense from the meat and all the vegetables. Green leafy vegetables such as spinach are a good source of vitamin K, essential for normal blood clotting.

1 SERVING: Calories 235; Fat 9g (Saturated 3g); Cholesterol 70mg; Sodium 1160mg; Carbohydrate 15g (Dietary Fiber 2g); Protein 26g **Food Exchanges:** 1 Starch; 3 Very Lean Meat; 1 Fat

Tomato–Lentil Soup

Prep Time: 10 Minutes   **Start to Finish:** 50 Minutes   **4 servings**

2
Carbohydrate
Choices

1 tablespoon olive or canola oil
1 large onion, finely chopped (1 cup)
1 medium stalk celery, cut into ½-inch pieces (½ cup)
2 cloves garlic, finely chopped
2 medium carrots, cut into ½-inch pieces (1 cup)
1 cup dried lentils (8 ounces), sorted and rinsed
4 cups water
2 teaspoons chicken or vegetable bouillon granules
1 teaspoon dried thyme leaves
¼ teaspoon pepper
1 dried bay leaf
1 can (28 ounces) diced tomatoes, undrained

1 Heat oil in 3-quart saucepan over medium-high heat. Cook onion, celery and garlic in oil about 5 minutes, stirring occasionally, until softened.

2 Stir in remaining ingredients except tomatoes. Heat to boiling; reduce heat. Cover and simmer 15 to 20 minutes or until lentils and vegetables are tender.

3 Stir in tomatoes. Simmer uncovered about 15 minutes or until heated through. Remove bay leaf.

Betty's Success Tip Lentils are so wholesome. They're low in calories and a good source of fiber, plus they're low in fat. Lentils are available in a variety of colors, including grayish brown (the most widely available), yellow and red. Use your favorite type of lentil in this easy soup.

1 SERVING: Calories 210; Fat 4g (Saturated 1g); Cholesterol 0mg; Sodium 950mg; Carbohydrate 43g (Dietary Fiber 14g); Protein 15g **Food Exchanges:** 1 Starch; 1 Very Lean Meat; 2 Vegetable

Easy Cheesy Vegetable Soup

Prep Time: 5 Minutes **Start to Finish:** 15 Minutes **5 servings**

3
Carbohydrate
Choices

4 ounces reduced-fat American cheese loaf, cubed

3½ cups fat-free (skim) milk

½ teaspoon chili powder

2 cups cooked brown or white rice

1 bag (1 pound) frozen cauliflower, carrots and asparagus (or other combination),
   thawed and drained

1 Heat cheese and milk in 3-quart saucepan over low heat, stirring occasionally, until cheese is melted.

2 Stir in chili powder. Stir in rice and vegetables; cook until hot.

Betty's Success Tip Be ready to make this soup anytime by cooking your favorite rice ahead of time. Store cooked rice in an airtight container or resealable plastic food-storage bag in the refrigerator up to 5 days or in the freezer up to 6 months.

1 SERVING: Calories 255; Fat 4g (Saturated 2g); Cholesterol 10mg; Sodium 460mg; Carbohydrate 44g (Dietary Fiber 4g); Protein 15g **Food Exchanges:** 2 Starch; 2 Vegetable; ½ Skim Milk

Smashed Potato Stew

2½
Carbohydrate
Choices

Prep Time: 10 Minutes   **Start to Finish:** 30 Minutes   **6 servings**

3½ cups fat-free (skim) milk
3 tablespoons all-purpose flour
1 tablespoon canola oil or butter
1 large onion, finely chopped (1 cup)
4 medium unpeeled potatoes (1½ pounds), cut into ¼-inch pieces
1 teaspoon salt
¼ teaspoon black pepper
⅛ teaspoon ground red pepper (cayenne)
1½ cups shredded reduced-fat sharp Cheddar cheese (6 ounces)
⅓ cup reduced-fat sour cream
8 medium green onions, sliced (½ cup)

1 Beat ½ cup of the milk and the flour with wire whisk until smooth; set aside. Heat oil in 4-quart Dutch oven over medium heat. Cook onion in oil about 2 minutes, stirring occasionally, until tender. Increase heat to high; stir in remaining 3 cups milk.

2 Stir in potatoes, salt, black pepper and red pepper. Heat to boiling; reduce heat. Simmer uncovered 15 to 16 minutes, stirring frequently, until potatoes are tender.

3 Beat in flour mixture with wire whisk. Cook about 2 minutes, stirring frequently, until thickened; remove from heat. Beat potato mixture with wire whisk until potatoes are slightly mashed. Stir in cheese, sour cream and green onions.

Betty's Success Tip This stew is so thick and creamy, you'll want to make it the star of your meal. At 2½ Carbohydrate Choices, you could partner it with a slice of crusty French bread and a fresh garden salad for a stick-to-your-ribs dinner.

1 SERVING: Calories 230; Fat 4g (Saturated 3g); Cholesterol 15mg; Sodium 670mg; Carbohydrate 36g (Dietary Fiber 3g); Protein 16g **Food Exchanges:** 2 Starch; ½ Skim Milk; 1 Very Lean Meat

VALUABLE VEGETABLES AND SALADS

Nut- and Fruit-Filled Squash

Prep Time: 15 Minutes **Start to Finish:** 1 Hour 5 Minutes **4 servings**

1 buttercup squash (2 to 2½ pounds)
¼ teaspoon salt
1 tablespoon butter or margarine, melted
1 cup Basic 4 cereal, coarsely crushed (½ cup)
1 teaspoon grated orange peel

1 Heat oven to 350°F. Cut squash into fourths; remove seeds and fibers. Place squash, cut sides up, in ungreased rectangular baking dish, 13 × 9 × 2 inches.

2 Sprinkle salt over squash. Pour water into baking dish until ¼ inch deep. Cover and bake 40 to 50 minutes or until tender.

3 Mix butter, cereal and orange peel; spoon into squash.

Betty's Success Tip Topping with a cereal that has nuts and dried fruit gives this squash sweetness and crunch. You can use Honey Nut Clusters or Harmony cereal instead, plus some dried raisins or cranberries.

1 SERVING: Calories 140; Fat 5g (Saturated 2g); Cholesterol 5mg; Sodium 250mg; Carbohydrate 26g (Dietary Fiber 6g); Protein 3g **Food Exchanges:** 1 Starch; 1 Fat

Creamy Confetti Succotash

Prep Time: 10 Minutes   **Start to Finish:** 20 Minutes   **5 servings**

1
Carbohydrate
Choices

1 tablespoon canola oil or butter
1 small red or green bell pepper, chopped (½ cup)
2 medium green onions, sliced (2 tablespoons)
2 cups fresh or frozen whole kernel corn
1 cup frozen baby lima beans
¼ cup half-and-half
2 teaspoons chopped fresh or ½ teaspoon dried marjoram leaves
¼ teaspoon salt
⅛ teaspoon pepper

1 Heat oil in 8-inch skillet over medium-high heat. Cook bell pepper and onions in oil 2 to 3 minutes, stirring occasionally, until crisp-tender.

2 Stir in remaining ingredients; reduce heat to medium-low. Cover and cook 5 to 6 minutes, stirring occasionally, until vegetables are tender.

Note from Dr. B Corn and lima beans are the essential ingredients in a succotash. Lima beans are a good source of protein, phosphorus, potassium, iron and fiber.

1 SERVING: Calories 115; Fat 4g (Saturated 2g); Cholesterol 10mg; Sodium 160mg; Carbohydrate 20g (Dietary Fiber 4g); Protein 4g **Food Exchanges:** 1 Starch; 1 Vegetable; ½ Fat

Creamy Confetti Succotash and
Breaded Pork Chops (page 55)

Corn- and Pepper-Stuffed Zucchini

1/2 Carbohydrate Choices

Prep Time: 10 Minutes   **Start to Finish:** 15 Minutes   **4 servings**

4 small zucchini (about 6 inches long)

1 tablespoon water

¾ cup frozen (thawed) whole kernel corn or cooled cooked fresh corn kernels

2 tablespoons diced red bell pepper

1 tablespoon chopped fresh or ½ teaspoon dried basil leaves

2 medium green onions, thinly sliced (2 tablespoons)

2 teaspoons olive or canola oil

⅛ teaspoon salt

1 Cut zucchini lengthwise in half; place zucchini and water in rectangular microwavable dish, 11 × 7 × 1½ inches. Cover with plastic wrap, folding back one edge or corner ¼ inch to vent steam.

2 Microwave on High 3 to 5 minutes or until zucchini is crisp-tender. When cool enough to handle, scoop centers from zucchini, leaving ¼-inch shells. Discard centers.

3 Mix remaining ingredients. Spoon about 2 tablespoons corn mixture into each zucchini shell.

Betty's Success Tip What's more versatile than veggies? You can turn them into flavorful side dishes or nibble on them raw for a fresh and crunchy low-carbohydrate snack. Try baby-cut carrots, pea pods, bell pepper or cucumber slices or celery sticks whenever you need a pick-me-up!

1 SERVING: Calories 65; Fat 3g (Saturated 0g); Cholesterol 0mg; Sodium 80mg; Carbohydrate 10g (Dietary Fiber 2g); Protein 2g **Food Exchanges:** 2 Vegetable; ½ Fat

Fresh Mozzarella and Tomatoes

0
Carbohydrate
Choices

Prep Time: 10 Minutes   **Start to Finish:** 3 Hours 10 Minutes   **8 servings**

4 medium tomatoes, cut into ¼-inch slices
¼ cup olive or canola oil
1 tablespoon chopped fresh or 1 teaspoon dried basil leaves
3 tablespoons red wine vinegar
1 tablespoon water
⅛ teaspoon salt
3 drops red pepper sauce
2 large cloves garlic, finely chopped
8 ounces fresh mozzarella cheese, sliced
Salad greens, if desired

1 Place tomatoes in glass or plastic dish. Shake remaining ingredients except cheese and salad greens in tightly covered container; pour over tomatoes.

2 Cover and refrigerate, turning tomatoes occasionally, at least 3 hours to blend flavors. Layer tomatoes alternately with cheese on salad greens.

Note from Dr. B Tomatoes are a good source of lycopene, a phytochemical (or naturally occurring plant chemical in foods) that may have cancer-fighting properties.

1 SERVING: Calories 150; Fat 12g (Saturated 4g); Cholesterol 15mg; Sodium 190mg; Carbohydrate 4g (Dietary Fiber 1g); Protein 8g **Food Exchanges:** 1 High-Fat Meat; 1 Vegetable; 1 Fat

Layered Gazpacho Salad

Prep Time: 15 Minutes   **Start to Finish:** 2 Hours 15 Minutes   **9 servings**

Lemon-Garlic Vinaigrette
½ cup olive or canola oil
¼ cup red wine vinegar
2 tablespoons lemon juice
1 teaspoon salt
¼ teaspoon pepper
1 clove garlic, finely chopped

Layered Gazpacho Salad
1 bag (8 ounces) Mediterranean lettuce blend
2 medium tomatoes, diced (2 cups)
2 medium cucumbers, diced (2 cups)
1 medium green bell pepper, chopped (1 cup)
½ cup finely chopped red onion
2 hard-cooked eggs, chopped
1 cup seasoned croutons

1 Shake all vinaigrette ingredients in tightly covered container. Place lettuce in large glass bowl. Layer tomatoes, cucumbers, bell pepper and onion on lettuce. Pour vinaigrette over top. Cover and refrigerate 1 to 2 hours to blend flavors.

2 Sprinkle eggs and croutons over salad. Toss before serving.

Note from Dr. B Tomatoes, green peppers and cucumbers give you a hefty dose of vitamins A and C in this tasty salad combination.

1 SERVING: Calories 165; Fat 14g (Saturated 2g); Cholesterol 45mg; Sodium 340mg; Carbohydrate 9g (Dietary Fiber 1g); Protein 3g **Food Exchanges:** 2 Vegetable; 3 Fat

Key Lime Fruit Salad

Prep Time: 15 Minutes   **Start to Finish:** 15 Minutes   **8 servings**

2 Carbohydrate Choices

1 container (6 ounces) Key lime pie–flavored artificially sweetened low-fat yogurt
2 tablespoons orange juice
2 cups fresh pineapple chunks
1 cup strawberry halves
2 cups green grapes
1 cup blueberries
2 cups cubed cantaloupe
¼ cup flaked or shredded coconut, toasted*

1 Mix yogurt and orange juice.

2 Layer fruit in order listed in 2½-quart clear glass bowl. Pour yogurt mixture over fruit. Sprinkle with coconut. Serve immediately.

*To toast coconut, heat in ungreased heavy skillet over medium-low heat 6 to 14 minutes, stirring frequently until browning begins, then stirring constantly until golden brown.

Betty's Success Tip Cut-up pineapple and cantaloupe, available in the produce section of your supermarket, can help shorten your chopping time. Save money by choosing fruits in season or feel free to substitute your favorites.

1 SERVING: Calories 120; Fat 2g (Saturated 1g); Cholesterol 0mg; Sodium 25mg; Carbohydrate 26g (Dietary Fiber 3g); Protein 2g **Food Exchanges:** 2 Fruit

DON'T FORGET DESSERTS

Fruit- and Nut-Topped Pound Cake,
Key Lime Bars (page 88) and
Oatmeal Brownies (page 89)

Fruit- and Nut-Topped Pound Cake

1½
Carbohydrate
Choices

Prep Time: 10 Minutes   **Start to Finish:** 15 Minutes   **14 servings**

1 package (10.75 ounces) frozen pound cake loaf, cut into fourteen ½-inch slices
⅔ cup soft cream cheese with strawberries, raspberries or pineapple
1 can (11 ounces) mandarin orange segments, well drained
1½ cups bite-size pieces assorted fresh fruit (kiwifruit, strawberry, raspberry, pear, apple)
½ cup reduced-fat chocolate-flavor syrup
½ cup sliced almonds

1 Set oven control to broil. Place pound cake slices on rack in broiler pan. Broil with tops 4 to 5 inches from heat 3 to 5 minutes, turning once, until light golden brown.

2 Spread each slice with about 2 teaspoons cream cheese. Cut slices diagonally in half to make 28 pieces. Top with orange segments and desired fresh fruit. Drizzle with syrup; sprinkle with almonds.

Betty's Success Tip This fruit and cake dessert can be drizzled with fat-free caramel or another ice-cream topping instead of the chocolate syrup. You can toast the pound cake up to a day ahead and assemble the cake slices and fruit up to 4 hours ahead. Cover and refrigerate until serving.

1 SERVING: Calories 190; Fat 11g (Saturated 4g); Cholesterol 35mg; Sodium 60mg; Carbohydrate 22g (Dietary Fiber 2g); Protein 3g **Food Exchanges:** 1 Starch; ½ Fruit; 2 Fat

Key Lime Bars

Prep Time: 15 Minutes **Start to Finish:** 4 Hours 20 Minutes **36 bars**

1
Carbohydrate
Choices

1½ cups graham cracker crumbs (20 squares)
⅓ cup butter or margarine, melted
3 tablespoons sugar
1 package (8 ounces) cream cheese, softened
1 can (14 ounces) sweetened condensed milk
¼ cup Key lime juice or regular lime juice
1 tablespoon grated lime peel
Additional lime peel, if desired

1 Heat oven to 350°F. Grease bottom and sides of square pan, 9 × 9 × 2 inches, with shortening. Mix cracker crumbs, butter and sugar thoroughly with fork. Press evenly in pan. Refrigerate while preparing cream cheese mixture.

2 Beat cream cheese in small bowl with electric mixer on medium speed until light and fluffy. Gradually beat in milk until smooth. Beat in lime juice and lime peel. Spread over layer in pan.

3 Bake about 35 minutes or until center is set. Cool 30 minutes. Cover loosely and refrigerate at least 3 hours until chilled. For bars, cut into 6 rows by 6 rows. Garnish with additional lime peel. Store covered in refrigerator.

Betty's Success Tip Graham cracker crumbs are used in this bar instead of high-calorie traditional cookie crumbs. Cutting calories and fat in little ways does add up; in fact, even a couple hundred fewer calories per day adds up to weight loss over time.

1 BAR: Calories 110; Fat 6g (Saturated 3g); Cholesterol 15mg; Sodium 70mg; Carbohydrate 12g (Dietary Fiber 0g); Protein 2g **Food Exchanges:** ½ Starch; ½ Fruit; 1 Fat

See photo on page 86.

Oatmeal Brownies

1 Carbohydrate Choices

Prep Time: 15 Minutes **Start to Finish:** 3 Hours 10 Minutes **48 brownies**

2½ cups old-fashioned or quick-cooking oats
¾ cup all-purpose flour
¾ cup packed brown sugar
½ teaspoon baking soda
¾ cup butter or margarine, melted
1 package (1 pound 6.5 ounces) supreme brownie mix with pouch of chocolate flavor syrup
⅓ cup water
⅓ cup canola or vegetable oil
2 or 3 eggs
½ cup chopped nuts

1 Heat oven to 350°F. Grease bottom only of rectangular pan, 13 × 9 × 2 inches, with shortening, or spray with cooking spray.

2 Mix oats, flour, brown sugar and baking soda in medium bowl; stir in butter. Reserve 1 cup of the oat mixture. Press remaining oat mixture in pan. Bake 10 minutes; cool 5 minutes.

3 Stir brownie mix, chocolate syrup, water, oil and 2 eggs for fudge-like brownies (or 3 eggs for cake-like brownies) in medium bowl, using spoon, until well blended. Stir in nuts. Spread over baked layer; sprinkle with reserved oat mixture.

4 Bake 35 to 40 minutes or until toothpick inserted 2 inches from side of pan comes out clean or almost clean. Cool completely, about 2 hours. For brownies, cut into 8 rows by 6 rows. Store tightly covered.

Note from Dr. B Use old-fashioned rolled oats often in your baking. Not only do they add flavor and texture to baked goods, they are also 100 percent whole grain. A recent study discovered that women who ate more whole-grain foods had lower rates of type 2 diabetes.

1 BROWNIE: Calories 135; Fat 6g (Saturated 3g); Cholesterol 15mg; Sodium 80mg; Carbohydrate 19g (Dietary Fiber 1g); Protein 2g **Food Exchanges:** 1 Starch; 1 Fat

See photo on page 86.

Creamy Vanilla–Caramel Cheesecake

Prep Time: 20 Minutes   **Start to Finish:** 5 Hours 5 Minutes   **16 servings**

15 reduced-fat chocolate or vanilla wafer cookies, crushed (½ cup)
2 packages (8 ounces each) reduced-fat cream cheese (Neufchâtel), softened
⅔ cup sugar
3 egg whites or ½ cup fat-free cholesterol-free egg product
2 teaspoons vanilla
2 cups vanilla low-fat yogurt
2 tablespoons all-purpose flour
⅓ cup fat-free caramel topping
Pecan halves, if desired

1 Heat oven to 300°F. Spray springform pan, 9 × 3 inches, with cooking spray. Sprinkle cookie crumbs over bottom of pan.

2 Beat cream cheese in medium bowl with electric mixer on medium speed until smooth. Add sugar, egg whites and vanilla. Beat on medium speed about 2 minutes or until smooth. Add yogurt and flour. Beat on low speed until smooth.

3 Carefully spread batter over cookie crumbs in pan. Bake 1 hour. Turn off oven; cool in oven 30 minutes with door closed. Remove from oven; cool 15 minutes. Cover and refrigerate at least 3 hours.

4 Drizzle caramel topping over cheesecake. Garnish with pecan halves. Store covered in the refrigerator.

Betty's Success Tip Cheesecake doesn't have to be high in fat and calories to be delicious. By replacing full-fat cream cheese and sour cream with their lower-fat counterparts, you can have your cheesecake—and eat it, too!

1 SERVING: Calories 175; Fat 7g (Saturated 5g); Cholesterol 25mg; Sodium 180mg; Carbohydrate 23g (Dietary Fiber 0g); Protein 5g **Food Exchanges:** 2 Carbohydrate; 1 Fat

Chocolate Dippers

Prep Time: 15 Minutes **Start to Finish:** 50 Minutes
12 to 16 servings (3 pieces each)

1 bag (6 ounces) semisweet chocolate chips (1 cup)
1 tablespoon shortening
3 to 4 dozen assorted dippers (dried apricots, strawberries, maraschino cherries, pretzels, small cookies, or angel food or pound cake cubes)
Colored sugar or candy decors, if desired

1 Line jelly roll pan, 15 × 10 × 1 inch, with waxed paper. Heat chocolate chips and shortening in heavy 1-quart saucepan over low heat, stirring frequently, until smooth; remove from heat.

2 Dip any of the assorted dippers ¾ of the way into chocolate; sprinkle with sugar. Place on waxed paper in pan.

3 Refrigerate uncovered about 30 minutes or until chocolate is firm.

Betty's Success Tip For Vanilla Dippers, use 6 ounces vanilla-flavored candy coating (almond bark), cut up, for the chocolate chips. To make Double Dippers, dip fruit into melted chocolate chips, then drizzle with melted vanilla-flavored candy coating or sprinkle with crushed candies.

1 SERVING: Calories 50; Fat 2g (Saturated 1g); Cholesterol 0mg; Sodium 25mg; Carbohydrate 7g (Dietary Fiber 1g); Protein 0g **Food Exchanges:** ½ Fruit; ½ Fat

Chocolate Snack Cake

Prep Time: 10 Minutes   **Start to Finish:** 1 Hour   **10 servings**

2
Carbohydrate
Choices

1½ cups all-purpose flour
1 cup sugar
¼ cup baking cocoa
1 teaspoon baking soda
½ teaspoon salt
⅓ cup canola or vegetable oil
1 teaspoon white vinegar
½ teaspoon vanilla
1 cup cold water

1 Heat oven to 350°F. Grease bottom and side of round pan, 9 × 1½ inches, or square pan, 8 × 8 × 2 inches, with shortening; lightly flour.

2 Mix flour, sugar, cocoa, baking soda and salt in medium bowl. Mix oil, vinegar and vanilla in measuring cup. Vigorously stir oil mixture and water into flour mixture about 1 minute or until well blended. Immediately pour into pan.

3 Bake 30 to 35 minutes or until toothpick inserted in center comes out clean. Cool 15 minutes. Serve warm.

Betty's Success Tip This cake tastes best when eaten warm. So try wrapping remaining pieces individually and warm in the microwave on High for 20 seconds for a 2-Carbohydrate-Choice snack.

1 SERVING: Calories 215; Fat 8g (Saturated 1g); Cholesterol 0mg; Sodium 240mg; Carbohydrate 357g (Dietary Fiber 1g); Protein 2g **Food Exchanges:** 2 Carbohydrate; 1½ Fat

Dear valued patient,

Welcome to our *Journey to a Better Health* loyalty program by Doctor Diabetic Supply. You have just embarked on a journey to achieving optimum health and better control of your diabetes. Not only are you getting your supplies from the largest independent Medicare supplier for diabetes supplies, you are receiving all the wonderful FREE benefits the program has to offer.

The benefits include:

- ✓ 100% Satisfaction guarantee
- ✓ Sample products and coupons
- ✓ Convenient home delivery with free shipping
- ✓ No up-front costs
- ✓ Your paperwork made easy
- ✓ Friendly reminders on reorders
- ✓ Trusted brand names available
- ✓ Educational material and newsletter
- ✓ Diabetes management program online that includes sample meal plans, nutritional and lifestyle tools, access to a dietitian and more.

Our mission is to help our patients live healthier lives by delivering quality products and unmatched service with every order. Doctor Diabetic Supply has served over 100,000 patients over the past year. Feel confident you are partnering with a brand name you can trust for a lifetime.

We hope you enjoy your free Betty Crocker Quick & Healthy Diabetes Recipes with delicious recipes for patients with diabetes.

Truly Yours,

Your friends at Doctor Diabetic Supply

89 NE 27th Street, Miami, FL 33137 ● 1-800-852-1652 ● www.doctordiabetic.com